REVEALING THE

by

Nicolas Stebbing CR

Mirfield Publications

Copyright © Nicolas Stebbing 2018

Published 2018 by Mirfield Publications
Community of the Resurrection
Stocksbank Road
Mirfield, West Yorkshire
WF14 0BN

www.mirfield.org.uk

Book Design by Bruce Carlin for Mirfield Publications.

British Library Cataloguing in Publication Data. A catalogue record for this book is available from the British Library.

ISBN 978-0-902834-47-7

REVEALING THE GOSPEL

Preface

The Bible is at the heart of Christian faith since it tells us about God and Jesus Christ. English people have had the Bible at the centre of their Christian life for at least four hundred years. Reading the Bible every day was a part of our Christian experience.

In the past fifty years this has become a problem for many. Scholars seem to have torn the Bible to pieces and cast doubt on whether it is true.

Some people react to this by ignoring modern scholarship, others by not reading the Bible at all. Both of these reactions are sadly wrong. Scholarship, properly done, enriches our experience of Scripture and deepens our faith in God.

This little collection of essays on the Gospels does not claim any great originality but sets out to share discoveries that I myself have found fascinating. If it encourages Anglicans to read more of the kind of biblical scholarship now available (in Rowan Williams' recent writing for instance) it will have fulfilled its purpose.

Nicolas Stebbing

CONTENTS

IS IT TRUE?

When we read the Bible as children we read it as any other story book, or set of teachings. We read the Gospels and take it for granted that this is what happened; this is what Jesus said. When we sit in church and listen to the readings from Scripture the same assumption is there: this is exactly how it happened; this is what Jesus said. It comes as quite a shock to find that most biblical scholars wouldn't agree with us. In fact most of our clergy wouldn't either, but if they say so they offend a large part of their congregation. So mostly they keep quiet until someone realises there is a problem and asks for help.

What is the problem and why should we doubt the truth of the Gospels? Well, in the first place the four Gospels do not always agree with each other. For instance, Matthew, Mark and Luke tell us that Jesus drove the money changers out of the temple just before he was arrested. John, however, puts this event right at the beginning of Jesus' ministry. Did Jesus do it twice? Or did one of the evangelists get it wrong? It may not really matter much except that it does mean not every event in the Gospel is exactly as described. Likewise, the first three evangelists place the Last Supper on the day of the Passover, and say it is a Passover meal; John puts it the day before and says it is not a Passover meal. John also says nothing about the institution of the Eucharist during that Supper. Instead he tells us about the washing of the disciples' feet. Did he not know about the Institution? If he did know (and he must have done) why did he leave it out?

We are on rather more important ground when it comes to the stories of the Resurrection. This is at the heart of our faith. If Christ was not raised from the dead then our faith is in vain, as St. Paul tells us. Well, we can say, we have several excellent stories of the disciples seeing Jesus after death. But do we? It is widely agreed that the last half of Chapter 16 in Mark's Gospel has been added afterwards. The Gospel really ends at 16:8. The women have found the tomb empty, they have been told to go and tell the disciples that Jesus has risen. But they do not see Jesus. Nor do they tell the disciples: 'they said nothing to anyone, for they were afraid.' The other three Gospels do give us some marvellous accounts of the disciples meeting the Risen Jesus. The difficulty there is that the accounts do not really agree. It is impossible to fit the various stories together. In Luke all the appearances of Jesus happen in or around Jerusalem whereas in Matthew and John some of them happen in Galilee. In Luke they all seem to happen on one day; in the other Gospels they are spread out over several weeks. Accidentally, or deliberately, someone has clearly got it wrong.

Or, finally there is the matter of Jesus' teaching. We are used to hearing it from the four different evangelists. Yet if we compare them we find they do not always agree. St Matthew gives us the Beatitudes (5:1-11). St Luke also gives us Beatitudes (6:20-23) but they are not the same. They do not actually contradict Matthew's version, but they are different. This happens over and over again in the Gospels. Sayings, stories and parables are recorded by two, three or even four evangelists, but there are differences between them. Do these differences matter? Is one of them completely accurate and the others less so? Does it matter? Does this make it uncertain whether everything we read in the gospels is true?

Or finally, what do we make of the long speeches Jesus gives? The Sermon on the Mount goes on for three full chapters. Did one of the disciples write it down as Jesus was talking? Or is it actually a collection of a whole lot of things Jesus said at different times, put together by Matthew himself? That is what most scholars now think. Or the wonderful Last Discourses in John (13-17); were these written down as it came out of Jesus' mouth? (Unlikely!) Did the disciple who wrote it up remember it accurately word for word under the inspiration of the Holy Spirit? Or did John himself compose most of it, based on his decades of reflection on the life and teaching of Jesus?

There are many more examples of difficulties, even contradictions in the Gospels as we have them. This much, however, is enough to show we have a problem. Are the Gospels really true? Can we trust what we read there to give us the real events of the life of Jesus, and the real substance of his teaching? If we can't be sure of that, have we lost the reasons for believing that Jesus is the Son of God, risen from the dead and bringing us salvation? Clearly this is not just an academic question; it is one that affects our whole salvation. We need to look at the possible answers to the question. As we do that we may find that what looks like an erosion of the grounds for Christian faith turns out to be a magnificent affirmation of it. When we look more deeply at these problems we begin to uncover a far more exciting drama than the one we are used to. So let us begin:

The first solution to this problem is to deny that there is a problem. We can say 'The Bible is true. The Holy Spirit has guaranteed this. Biblical scholars are simply making difficulties for faith. There is no error in the Bible and any apparent errors can be explained, or they are a sign of our lack of faith.' That is actually what many faithful Christians do say. Unfortunately, it involves a lot of rather specious argument. It also means that we are applying a different set of rules to our Christian life from that of our ordinary life. That involves us in a contradiction which is not good for us. Most seriously, I think, it prevents us digging deeper into the world of Scripture and discovering a much more lively and exciting faith in Christ.

To do this we need to understand the process by which the Gospels came to be written. This involves working backwards in a number of steps:

i.   The Gospels are written in Greek, but Jesus himself spoke Aramaic. So did all his first disciples. This means the Gospels have already been through at least one translation process and that alone may account for some of the differences between them.

ii. The Gospels as we have them probably came into their final form between 65 and 90 AD, that is between 30 and 50 years after the death of Christ. In the years after Christ died it is clear that stories about him circulated amongst the believers. Sometimes these stories were written down, but in an age when only a small minority could read and write most of these stories circulated in oral form. As they circulated little changes occurred. Oral tradition can actually be very accurate in its substance and sometimes in the very wording, but there is always a tendency to improve the story, to make it a bit more dramatic, to change the wording so that it can be more easily remembered. This would account for a number of the differences between the various stories and teaching in the Gospels.

iii. That may seem to suggest the stories are wrong; in fact, the agreement between the different accounts is surprisingly close. What is really exciting is to see in our imagination hundreds of Christians from those first few years, excitedly telling each other the stories as they had heard them. Probably they argued with each other, corrected each other and discussed the significance of these stories. It only takes a little imagination for us to see that we are in touch with this very early conversation and can take part in it.

iv. It seems very clear that Mark's Gospel was the first one written down and that Matthew and Luke used it. Sometimes they both used it exactly as it was written. On other occasions they changed the text. The fascinating thing is that one can often see that they each had consistent reasons for changing the text of Mark. Sometimes it was just to improve Mark's rather rough

Greek. Other times it was in order to present the Gospel of Jesus in a slightly different way. Again this makes us see that each Gospel as we have it is not an impartial, factual account of the life and teaching of Jesus, but the account of four very different Christians, living in different places, at different times and with different understandings of the message of Jesus. Their differences hardly ever contradict, but they put the emphasis in different places. In this way they produce a much more interesting and multi-layered Gospel of Our Lord Jesus Christ. Some of these differences will be explored in the chapters that follow.

There is a danger with all holy things that we can turn them into false gods, that is gods which replace the real God. God is infinite and we cannot control him. The Jews knew this, but were always tempted to make statues of him that could be controlled. This would make God safe and remove the uncertainty of believing in a living God who kept saying new things. We can do the same. We can tie God up in the Bible, limit what he may say to what we find there and refuse to interpret the Bible in a way that gives us an uncomfortable, challenging God. We can do the same with the Church, the Sacraments or anything else in our Christian tradition. We can set them in concrete, insist that only one definition of them is true and refuse to recognise God anywhere else. Then the gift that God has given us becomes a false God that prevents us from hearing the real God speak. If we allow modern scholarship to take the Bible apart and raise questions about its meaning we can actually be letting the Holy Spirit in to our reading of Scripture. That makes it much more exciting.

As Christians we do not believe finally in the Bible or even in the Gospels. We believe in our Lord Jesus Christ and in his Father who sent him to us. The Bible and the gospels are a wonderful witness to God and to Christ, but neither God nor Christ are imprisoned within its pages. God is active now, in his Holy Spirit. Christ is risen from the dead and alive to us today. We need to free ourselves from too close a dependence on the literal truth of the Bible if we are to be people who are completely centred on Christ. This is why it is so important to dig into the text of the Gospels to try and find the Christ whom the Gospel writers themselves are trying to present to us. But this is not simply an attempt to look back through a telescope to what happened 2,000 years ago. Christ is alive today and we can depend on him to come to us today as we read the Scriptures. We need to hear Christ speaking, let him give new meaning to the words and let him show us what they say to us now. We are concerned ultimately with the present, not the past.

John in his Gospel has Jesus tell us "when the Spirit of truth comes he will guide you into all truth." (Jn 16:13) The early Christians had a very intense experience of the spirit of Christ, as do many Christians today. It is fundamental to our Christian faith that the Spirit has been constantly active in Christian life, preserving the Church from fundamental error (though many mistakes have been made). Part of this is activity of the Spirit is the formation of Scripture. The Spirit was there with the first Christians guiding them in preserving the sayings and events of Jesus' life. He was there in the first writings of the Gospel and he was there in the translations. He remains with us now in the study and interpretation of the Scriptures. This does not mean that every word we say or think about Scripture is true, but that he is present in us and with us as we seek the meaning of Scripture and try to let God's voice come to us through it. Reading Scripture with an awareness of the problems and the many different voices in it, calls us to listen to the Spirit and to rely on his presence in us to bring us to Christ.

CHILDHOOD STORIES

The stories of the childhood of Jesus are perhaps the most beautiful and best loved stories of the whole Bible. They are the main part of our celebration of Christmas and have enriched us with wonderful paintings, music, carols and devotion to the Christ child. Yet, curiously, only two of the Gospel writers, Matthew and Luke, record them. Mark and John don't mention the birth of Jesus. And, even more curiously, the stories given by Matthew and Luke are almost completely different. Very little of the one is contained in the other. This makes us ask, did they not know each other's stories? Was there a reason why they selected and used the ones they did? There is of course a third possibility, that they simply made up the stories to suit their own purpose. That is possible but the evidence is that the stories were around before Matthew and Luke got hold of them. They certainly touched them up, but they didn't write them from scratch.

What they agree on is:

- Both agree that Jesus was born in Bethlehem, though Matthew seems to assume the family were living there, whereas Luke had to get them there by means of the Emperor Augustus census.

- Both agree that Jesus spent most of his childhood in Nazareth where the family lived, though Matthew suggests they went there to get away from the area ruled by Herod's son.

- Both agree that an angel announced the coming of Jesus, though in Matthew the angel speaks to Joseph in a dream, while Luke has the angel speak to Mary face to face.

- Both agree that Mary is the mother of Jesus and Joseph her betrothed husband. Matthew makes it clear that Joseph is not the father of Jesus and that God is. In Luke it is clear that God is involved in this birth, though it is possible that Joseph was still the human father. We will later find that Matthew has a higher Christology than Luke; that is, Jesus is emphatically the Son of God from the start.

- Both agree that it is the angel who gives the child the name Jesus, though Matthew's angel offers also the name Emmanuel, never again used in the New Testament, which is odd.

That really is all there is of exact agreement in the stories the two evangelists offer. There are however, some general agreements:

- Both writers include a genealogy of Jesus. Unfortunately the genealogies are very different; Matthew traces Jesus back to Abraham; Luke takes him back to Adam. On the way they use many different characters: Joseph's father is Jacob in Matthew and Heli in Luke. Both genealogies do include David as an ancestor of Joseph, to establish that Jesus is of the family of David, yet that in itself is odd since Matthew makes it clear that Joseph is not the father of Jesus and it is possible that Luke thinks the same.

- Both writers show people from outside the family circle visiting Jesus soon after his birth, recognising that this child was an extraordinary gift from God. However the visitors come from almost opposite ends of the social scale. In Matthew they are wise men from the East; in Luke they are shepherds from the fields nearby.

And that really is that. It is hard to discern any other points of contact between the rest of the stories in the period before Jesus was baptised by John.

That leaves us with three possibilities: either the evangelists were using the only stories they had; or they chose the stories that best suited the kind of Gospel they wanted to tell; or they simply made up the stories in order to suit their purpose. The second and third possibilities make the same fundamental point, that Matthew and Luke are not just filling a gap with pious stories. They wanted these stories to prepare us for the Gospel which was to come. And indeed we find the stories full of the particular concerns which each of these writers has in his Gospel.

To examine these stories adequately would require several books. Here we can only pick out the salient concerns of the two evangelists:

Matthew: The Genealogy (1:1-17)

There are two interesting points about this:

  i. It traces the descent of Jesus back to Abraham. Matthew, of all the evangelists seems to have the greatest concern as to how the Christian Gospel relates to the Jews. This complex question is handled in a number of different ways in his Gospel. Here he is asserting that Jesus was a Jew, from the very heart of Judaism and his line of descent from Abraham goes through David, the greatest Jewish king.

ii. Yet Matthew inserts into that genealogy four women before he gets to Mary: Tamar, Rahab, Ruth and Bathsheba (not actually named). It is unusual for women to be included in a genealogy and each of these women raise a question: Tamar seduced her father in law Judah in order to get justice; Rahab was not Jewish and was a prostitute in Jericho, though she acquired hero status in the Jewish pantheon by helping the Jews to conquer Jericho, making her a traitor to her own people; Ruth is one of the most virtuous and impressive women in the whole Old Testament, yet she was not Jewish; she was a Moabite, a despised neighbouring people; and Bathsheba, also the wife of a foreigner, Uriah the Hittite, was a constant reminder of David's most famous infidelity and shame.

Matthew: Joseph and Mary (1:18 – 25)

Of the many different points that could be culled from this story we may choose just three:

i. Jesus, the son of the most pure, most holy God, began his life in scandal. His mother was pregnant and this could only be blamed on Mary's betrothed husband jumping the gun, or another man. This exposed Mary to public disgrace and the danger of stoning, the punishment for adultery prescribed by the law. Matthew's gospel constantly raises the matter of Jesus' relationship with the law, and ends with Jesus himself killed and in disgrace.

ii. Joseph is described as 'righteous', 'just' or 'upright', depending on the translation. At first sight this suggests that Joseph would uphold the law either to have Mary stoned or at least publicly disgraced. In fact he intends to 'dismiss her privately' and when told by the angel to marry her, goes ahead willingly and cares for her son. In that respect he reflects the justice of God, who does not actually inflict the punishment of the law on his people but shows endless compassion and mercy.

iii. Jesus will save his people from their sins. This promise would have created a number of possible expectations: that he will save them from the result of their sins, that is, their occupation by the foreign power of Rome; that he will save them from sin itself, making them law abiding so that the society they live in will be peaceful and just; or that he will free them from sin so that they can pass through death, the punishment for sin, and enter into the life of God. The Gospel Matthew writes shows the second two options, rather than the first, are the reason for Jesus' coming.

Matthew: Herod and the Magi (2:1-12)

'After Jesus had been born at Bethlehem in Judea in the reign of Herod...' Curiously the actual birth of Jesus is not described, only the response to it of two opposing groups: the Magi, wise men from the mythical east come to worship; and Herod 'and all Jerusalem' who are thrown into consternation. Historically, this is ambiguous. Herod was widely hated by pious Jews, but would all Jerusalem really have known of the mission of the Magi? Matthew, however, wants us to know at the start that all Jerusalem will reject Jesus in the end. Indeed he will be crucified there. By contrast the Gentiles, represented here by the wise men, will accept Jesus and worship him as king. From this story we may gather four important points:

i. Jesus is revealed at once as Christ and the Magi come to him to lay at his feet all their wealth and knowledge; magic and human wisdom is replaced by the light of divine truth.

ii. The coming of the Magi reflects the Old Testament tradition that Gentiles will come to Jerusalem (Zechariah 8:23); also the future history that it will be the Gentiles, not the people of Jerusalem who will recognise Christ;

iii. Matthew teaches us here that the proper response to Jesus is worship and offering the best we have;

iv. The Magi discover the whereabouts of Jesus not by their own cleverness nor by human advice but by the guidance of God. The symbol of the star leading them onwards has remained powerfully significant to us ever since.

Matthew: The Flight into Egypt and the massacre of the children (2:13-23)

Did this happen? The Jewish historian Josephus, was anxious to record every bad deed of Herod, yet he makes no mention of this. On the other hand it was the kind of thing Herod would have done. For Matthew it provides the pretext for sending Jesus off to Egypt and bringing him back to Nazareth (where he was known to have grown up) rather than Bethlehem which would have been more logical. It seems that Matthew, unlike Luke, did not know that the Holy Family actually came from Nazareth. Egypt was a common place for Jews to flee to. Throughout the Old Testament people in disgrace or danger ran away to Egypt. There was a very thriving Jewish community in Egypt so it was a natural place for Jews to flee to. The story of the flight to Egypt is plausible even if it cannot be proved.

Matthew, however, is not primarily concerned with history. He sees in this story a number of parallels between Jesus who delivered humanity from the power of sin and Moses who delivered Israel from the power of Egypt. Jesus was rescued from the slaughter of the babies in Bethlehem as Moses was rescued from the slaughter of the Hebrew children in Egypt. Jesus flees into Egypt to escape the anger of the tyrant Herod, just as Moses fled from Egypt to escape the anger of Pharaoh. Moses returned from the desert to Egypt to rescue his people from the power of Pharaoh. Jesus comes out of Egypt to rescue his people from the power of the evil one. The slaughter of the innocents foreshadows the killing of Jesus who was innocent, too. Egypt for the Jews was both a place of slavery and also a place from which rescue from political tyrants sometimes came. And Hosea 11:1, 'Out of Egypt I called my son', provides a biblical foretelling of this event.

At one point at least Matthew is historically well informed: Archelaus was the cruellest of Herod's sons. Galilee was certainly a safer place to live than Judea.

Luke's Stories

Once again we may look at Luke's infancy stories by asking ourselves how they prepare us for the Gospel that is to come.

i.   **Jerusalem**. In Luke's Gospel Jerusalem plays a very important role. The whole story of Jesus describes him moving from Galilee to Jerusalem where he is crucified and where also he rises from the dead. Then in Acts the story moves out from Jerusalem to the whole world. So we find in the first few Chapters that John's birth is announced in Jerusalem though his birth takes place in the country. The birth of Jesus is announced in the country district of Galilee, but takes place in Judea and he is presented in the temple, the sacred heart of Jerusalem.

ii.   **Mary.** In Matthew's stories Mary plays a largely passive role. The focus is on Joseph and then on Jesus. In Luke Mary is the central character. The annunciation is made to her; she visits Elizabeth and proclaims the Magnificat; she appears in each of the stories of Jesus and she is given the particular role of 'pondering these words in her heart' (2: 19,51). Not only does Mary play this great role in the stories, but Elizabeth, another woman, has a strong supporting role as the first to recognise who this child is that Mary is carrying. In the First Century Jewish women stayed out of the limelight, quietly at home. Luke, however, gives them a different role. In the Infancy narratives they are two of the major players (Anna also is a third). Throughout Luke's Gospel we will find that stories about women appear constantly after stories about men. Luke appears to be telling us that in the new Christian order that he is part of, women have a status equal to that of men.

iii. **The Poor.** Luke shows a particular concern for the poor. In Jesus' opening speech about his mission he says clearly that he has come to preach the good news to the poor (4:18). In Luke's version of the Beatitudes it is simply the poor, (not the poor in spirit) who will have the Kingdom of God (6:20). In the story of the birth of Jesus it is the humble and much despised shepherds who receive the news. Joseph and Mary are presented as poor parents who can only offer a pair of turtle doves for the Presentation of Jesus in the Temple. Mary in her Magnificat tells how God has "looked with favour on his lowly servant" and how he will "fill the hungry with good things." By contrast the rich will be sent away empty, the powerful will be pulled down from their thrones while the humble are lifted up. Luke is offering a revolutionary Gospel which is definitely good news for the poor. Throughout the Old Testament, in the law and particularly in the prophets God proclaims his concern for the poor who are constantly exploited by the rich. Luke has the same concern.

iv. **Israel.** The Angel tells Zechariah that his son "will turn many of the people of Israel to the Lord their God." (1:16) Zechariah in his turn praises God that he has looked favourably on his people (1:68) that he has raised up another David and that he has remembered the promises made to Abraham. Mary meanwhile also praises God for helping his servant Israel according to his promise to Abraham. The angel has also told Mary that Jesus will have the throne of David and will rule over the house of Jacob. Later, Simeon describes him as "a glory to your people Israel." (2:32) Luke wants to show that Jesus was not intended to displace the people of Israel from their promised inheritance; rather he is the fulfilment of all these promises. The difference now is that the Gentiles are taken into this promise. The light will go out to all nations. But that too is in accordance with at least one strand of the prophets' teaching.

v. **Holy Spirit.** John the Baptist is described as filled with the Holy Spirit; it is the Holy Spirit who will come upon Mary and give her a son who will be the Messiah; Elizabeth in 1:41 is filled with the Holy Spirit so that she can recognise Jesus; Zechariah is filled with the Holy Spirit when he speaks his Song of thanksgiving. The Holy Spirit rests on Simeon, reveals that he will not die without seeing the Messiah, and leads him into the temple to meet Jesus.

vi. **Suffering.** In all this joy there is a note of suffering: "The child is destined for the falling and rising of many in Israel…" Can this be a reference to the catastrophe of the destruction of Jerusalem which will come on those who have rejected Jesus? He will be a sign that will be opposed and a sword will pierce Mary's heart also. (2:34,35) On the beginning of the story, as with Matthew's infancy stories, the shadow of the passion falls.

In both Matthew and Luke the stage is now set and the theology has been prepared for the telling of the story of Jesus.

JESUS, THE SON OF GOD – IN MATTHEW

Christians today believe that Jesus is the Son of God, and we have believed this since the earliest days of our faith, but not quite from the beginning. For a Jew it was impossible to believe that anyone could be truly and completely God's son, because that would mean there were two Gods. It was a fundamental tenet of Jewish religion that there was only one God. So in the gospels we see people struggle with this new idea. Is Jesus the Messiah? The son of David? Some kind of heavenly messenger? Can he really be God? Each of the Gospel writers presents this struggle slightly differently. Each is convinced that Jesus is the Son of God but draws out this mystery in different ways. What does Matthew make of this?

Matthew uses the phrase eight times in 28 Chapters. However, before we look at those we need to see how from the beginning of his Gospel Matthew makes very clear his own (and the Christian Church's) belief that Jesus is the Son of God. In 2:15 he suggests the real significance of the flight of the Holy Family into Egypt is that Jesus can then come out of Egypt and fulfil the prophecy of Hosea, 'Out of Egypt I have called my son.' Then in 3:17 at the Baptism of Jesus a voice came from heaven saying, "This is my beloved Son." What is interesting here is that Matthew has changed what he received from Mark. In Mark 1:11 the voice from heaven says, "You are my beloved son." This may suggest that Jesus did not yet know this, or needed to be confirmed in what he thought was his vocation. In Matthew it is not Jesus who is addressed. Jesus is in no doubt who he is. It is the crowds, and us, who are told whom we are meeting for the first time.

The seven other occasions when the title is used of Jesus are interesting, and unexpected. The first two are in 4:3 and 4:6 during the temptation in the wilderness. They occur therefore on the lips of the Devil. There is an ambiguity here. Is the Devil tempting Jesus to doubt whether he is the Son of God? Or is he tempting him to misuse the powers that come to him as Son of God. At any rate it would appear the Devil knows who he is. Matthew has arranged matters so that the first two texts which tell us who Jesus is (without actually using the title) are from God. The second two are from the Devil. The next is also from devils, in this case the demons who possess the Gadarene demoniacs in 8:29. Only in 14:33 do we finally get the confession on the lips of Jesus' disciples in the boat, after they have seen Jesus walk on water. This is followed up two chapters later by Peter in 16:16 who makes the fullest declaration of the divine sonship of Jesus, "You are the Christ, the son of the living God." That is a very Jewish description of God and makes it clear that this is not a pagan concept of a son of a god (of whom there were many) but the one and only Son of the one and only true God.

The next appearance of the title is on the lips of the High Priest Caiaphas who puts Jesus on oath to say whether or not he is 'the Christ, the Son of God.' (26:63) Then again it is spoken by those who mock Jesus at the crucifixion. Here it occurs twice (27:40,43).

The first is "If you are the Son of God", the second, 'He said, "I am the Son of God."' The first form is of course identical to that of Satan in his temptations.

Finally the phrase appears after the death of Jesus, on the lips of the Roman centurion, "Truly, this was the Son of God." (27:54)

What more can we say of these verses in which the title 'Son of God' appears?

The first two uses of the title on the lips of the devil are clearly a temptation to Jesus. We may not be quite sure of the force of the temptation; is the devil trying to get Jesus to doubt that he is the Son of God? If he doubts it he might then do some mighty works to prove to himself that he is who he thinks he is. In this he would be attempting to manipulate God himself instead of trusting what God had revealed to him. Alternatively, Satan could be tempting Jesus to push the edges of his understanding of his divine nature into areas which were not legitimate. The Son of God may have the same infinite power that God himself has; this does not mean he can use it either to feed himself when he is hungry, or to jump safely off a high building. Jesus knows this and knows therefore that accepting the devil's challenge would be disobedience to his Father, and a failure to trust. For any son the crux of his relationship with his father is trusting obedience; that is what love is. Matthew in his Gospel presents this trusting obedience as the defining characteristic of the sonship of Jesus. This is then taken up in the third temptation when Satan offers Jesus the whole world if he will worship him. The choice for Jesus now is clear: obedience to the Father, or obedience to Satan. He does not fail the test.

That seems to be the primary meaning of these temptations, but a secondary interpretation may also have been in Matthew's mind; that is, our own tendency to misinterpret the meaning of 'Son of God' and try to make the Son of God in the image we should like him. This was a temptation for the contemporaries of Jesus, to see the Messiah either as a wonderworker, or better, as a person whose prime work was to heal the sick, raise the dead, cast out demons and generally make the world a pain free place to live in. Jesus did many of those things and they had an important role in revealing the kind of Messiah he was to be. That was not, however, the main role of the Son of God. Likewise the temptation to jump off the roof of the temple was a temptation to fit a human idea of godly power – to fly, to move through space, to defy gravity. Greek gods did all these things, but human beings could not do them. If Jesus had done them he would have denied his humanity, and his human nature was a crucial part of his purpose in being among men. In the end we see these temptations, along with the third as being our own temptation from which Christians have always suffered, and into which they have very often fallen, to recast Jesus as our own ideal Messiah – a healer of all diseases, a political conqueror, a human rights activist, a moral reformer. Each of these roles have a place in his messianic ministry, but for Jesus to be caught in any one of them, or indeed in the sum of all of them, would seriously miss the point and turn him into a false god, who distracted people's attention from the real God. And that could not be.

Believing that Jesus was the Son of God was not (and still is not) the main issue at stake in Christian conversion. Evidently Satan believed Jesus was the Son of God. So, too, did the demons possessing the men of Gadara (8:29). We are reminded of James 2:19, 'The devils believe, and tremble.' These devils also acknowledged right away the power the Son of God had over them. They begged him not to send them away or destroy them, recognising that he could do this. Jesus pays no attention to their pleas. He is not going to negotiate with them or enter into discussion with them. His power is absolute; he sends them into the pigs which cast themselves into the water and evidently destroy the demons, or at least rid the neighbourhood of them. The ancient world had different views of the powers of demons. It was probable that some saw Jesus as on a par with the demons, having the same degree of power. His power was good; theirs was bad. If they came into contact it would be as two equally matched champions fighting for the souls of particular men and women. Had Jesus simply been an angel that may have been so. As God he is not equal to devils, neither to Satan, the prince of all devils, or to a whole legion of devils as we have at Gadara. He is completely and unambiguously above them. This story makes it clear that Jesus is not just a divine creature with some amazing divine powers. He is, quite simply God with the absolute power that a true Son of the one and only God can wield.

Our next use of the title comes in 14.33, after the disciples have witnessed Jesus walking on the water. The story is one which has layers of meaning for the Christian Church. Early in Christian history the boat came to be seen as a symbol of the Church, with its little body of faithful Christians adrift in a stormy and dangerous sea. Jesus comes to them out of this sea and brings them safety. In Matthew the episode involving Peter is most fully developed. He asks to walk with Jesus on the water and is granted his request, and he can walk for a while. But when his faith fails him he needs Jesus to support him. Clearly the first layer of meaning is simply that Jesus must be divine to be able to walk on water. So it is not surprising that the disciples tell him, "Truly, you are the son of God." This is the first and only time all the disciples say that. However, Greek and other pagan gods could do such things as walk on water, or fly through the sky. What is unusual about Jesus is that he shares this power with one who is not a god. Why should it be Peter? Peter is shown throughout Matthew's Gospel to be the leader of the disciples. Peter loves Jesus and for this reason wants to share everything that Jesus experiences, even his cross. Peter's words are interesting. He says, "Order me to come to you." (14:28) and Jesus simply says "Come!" and Peter comes. Obedience is all. As long as Peter's trust in Jesus is absolute his obedience is absolute and he is like Jesus in his own obedience to his Father. When the trust fails, so does the likeness. Jesus is Son of God, not just because of his power over physical things, but because of his trustworthy love which gives his disciples a unique relationship with him.

Although all the disciples in this story confess that Jesus is the son of God, only Peter walks on the water. So it is not surprising that in the next confession of Jesus' divine sonship it is Peter who speaks on behalf of the disciples and says, "You are the Christ, the Son of the living God." (16:16). In this, the fullest proclamation of the divinity of Jesus (both Christ and Son of God) Matthew appears to have expanded the story he received from Mark. In Mark Peter simply confesses Jesus is the Christ. This could confuse him with Jewish expectations of a political messiah. It does not say he is divine. Matthew takes Jesus out of the political arena; he places him firmly in the religious sphere, and by adding the epithet 'most high' to God he makes it clear that this is the Jewish God who is alone and supreme. Jesus is not the son of some lesser deity, a kind of Hercules or Achilles who could do great things because of his divine blood. Being son of the Jewish God makes him also God. That was a huge claim to make, unacceptable to any orthodox Jew. In the end it was the claim that marked out the Christian faith from its Jewish parent and by Matthew's own day had led to an acrimonious parting of the ways.

Now that the disciples have openly recognised who Jesus is we would expect the title to appear quite often. In fact it does not. Matthew rations it carefully to make a particular point. The next occasion is not until Jesus is on the Cross. Here it is the passers by who tempt him "If you are the Son of God, come down from the cross." (27:40) and in v.43 it is the chief priests who tell him to prove his divinity "for he said, I am the Son of God." The words in 27:40 are of course exactly those which Satan used in the desert. And the fact that the bystanders use the title twice reflects, without exactly copying, the devil's use of it twice on that occasion. It is impossible not to see the bystanders tempting Jesus in the place of the devil. And they are tempting him in the same way as the devil did, to use his divine power to escape from the course which the Father wanted for him. It is Jesus' obedience as a son to his heavenly father that is being tested, but it also reflects what he himself said in 16:25 "Whoever wishes to save his life, will lose it…" Jesus cannot deny himself and goes to his death.

Then comes the final use of the title by the centurion after the death of Jesus: "Truly, this was the Son of God." (27:54). The significance here is that it is a gentile who makes this confession of faith. Just before this the Jewish passers by and the Jewish high priests, and scribes and elders (Matthew leaves no one out) have used the title to mock Jesus and proclaim their unbelief in him. Now a gentile has proclaimed his divine sonship. It is a clear indication of which way the Gospel will go, and coming as it does, after its two uses by the tempters it seems to correspond to the words God spoke to the crowd at Jesus' baptism. "This is my beloved son."

This brings us to a final look at Matthew's artistry. One of the common rhetorical devices used in the ancient world was that of *inclusio*, that is, using particular words, phrases or ideas as brackets within a piece of writing in order to heighten their effect. This is what Matthew has done. If we list the occurrences of this title from the opening of the ministry of Jesus we find it:

3:17	on the lips of God
4:3 & 6	from the tempter in the desert
8:29	from the demons at Gadara
14:33 & 16:16	on the lips of his disciples

26:63	by Caiaphas
27:40 & 43	from his tempters at the cross
27:54	on the lips of the gentile centurion.

There is a very neat pattern:

1. God.
2. Twice from the devil tempting him to disobey God.
3. From demons acknowledging, despite their wickedness, that he is Son of God.
4. Twice from his disciples.
5. From Caiaphas (like the demons) saying what was in fact true.
6. Twice from bystanders (like the devil) tempting him to disobey God.
7. From the centurion effectively repeating the voice from heaven at the start.

Clearly, though Matthew has used the title only eight times, it is one that is of great importance to him: he uses it to frame his entire Gospel, to bring out the contrast between those who tempt Jesus to disobey his Father, and the disciples who learn to enter into sonship with the Father by obeying Jesus; he shows how the revelation of Jesus' divine sonship by the Father at the beginning of the story is finally taken up at the end by a gentile, representing all those gentiles who by Matthew's own time are taking the Gospel out into the world. And it is here we get our final *inclusio*: in 2:15 we saw how Matthew has God bring his Son from Egypt into Israel to deliver his people. At the end of the Gospel we see Jesus go back to Galilee, which is almost Gentile country in the eyes of Jerusalem, and send his disciples out into the whole world to take the Gospel there (28:16-20). The story is now complete.

MARK - THE FIRST CHAPTER

Mark's Gospel is an extraordinary piece of writing. It is the shortest Gospel, only sixteen chapters, and the first to be written. Mark is thought to have been a bit less educated than Matthew or Luke. His Greek is rougher, but very direct. Yet both Matthew and Luke clearly thought highly of his writing since they used most of what he wrote as a basis for their own gospels.

One interesting way of getting an idea of the message Mark wanted to put out is to look at the first chapter alone. It is astonishing how much Mark packs into forty five verses:

i.   John the Baptist appears,

ii.   Jesus is baptised,

iii. Jesus goes into the wilderness,

iv. Jesus begins his ministry,

v.   Jesus calls the first disciples

vi. Jesus casts out a demon

vii. Jesus heals Peter's mother in law,

viii. Jesus heals 'all who were sick or possessed.'

ix. Jesus goes preaching throughout all Galilee,

x.   Jesus heals a leper,

xi. Jesus is surrounded by crowds so he can no longer go into towns.

Mark emphasises the speed at which things are happening by introducing almost every event with 'and immediately'. In the rest of the Gospel things slow down a bit, but the impression is still of Jesus moving fast, gathering great crowds, performing lots of miracles. Jesus seems to be making a huge impression on the people of Judea and Galilee.

Then the message:

Mark is unambiguous: the first verse describes Jesus as Son of God. In the Gospel itself the disciples take a long time to work this out (Chapter 8) and the people, despite their enthusiasm for the miracles and the teaching never really get it. But we know from the start that this is what Mark wants to show us.

Then John the Baptist appears, preaching a baptism of repentance and forgiveness. This is important for it is clearly the message Jesus himself took up. In v. 15 he says "Repent, and believe in the Gospel". For both John and Jesus 'repent' means to turn towards God and that means turning away from every kind of sin. But what does Jesus mean when he tells people to 'believe in the Gospel'? Well, gospel simply means good news, and John the Baptist has already told us what that is: "After me comes he who... will baptise you with the Holy Spirit." Quite what that means is never really spelled out, but it does mean that this person Jesus will have about him the power of God and that is what we see in the miracles that come so thick and fast.

The miracles tell us one really important thing about Jesus: he has an astonishing power from God. In describing them Mark keeps using words like 'amazed' which show how people reacted to these miracles. The miracles are Mark's main proof that Jesus comes from God. That, as we have seen is the core of this Good News, that Jesus, Son of God, has come into the world and is telling everybody to turn back to God. The people never really understand this, but the demons do. Here, and elsewhere in the Gospel, the demons recognise Jesus for who he is: "I know who you are, the Holy One of God." cries the demon in 1.24.

The first miracle, casting out this demon, takes place in a synagogue on the Sabbath. At this point the fact it is the Sabbath causes no comment. Later, in Chapter 3, it does cause trouble as people criticise him for doing work on the Sabbath. Mark makes the point in the very first miracle that Jesus is greater than the Sabbath because he came from God.

Jesus does not do miracles just to show off his power. It is Mark who draws attention to the power which Jesus must have to perform these healings. Jesus himself regularly tries to downplay them; he tells people to keep silent. In that first miracle Jesus actually starts by teaching the people and they were 'astonished by his teaching for he taught them as one who had authority.' (1.22) The miracle which follows then serves to underline this authority and show that Jesus is not just a very clever or persuasive rabbi; his authority comes from God. Later in the Chapter we see what is, perhaps, Jesus' own best motive for healing people: 'Moved with pity…' That in itself is part of his claim to be the Son of God. The God of Israel was not a cold, distant, intellectual sort of God. He was warm, passionate and cared about his people. Throughout the Old Testament he is shown to care for the poor, 'the widow, the orphan and the stranger.' He had compassion on his people when they were slaves in Egypt and brought them out. He had compassion on them when they were in exile in Babylon and brought them home.

Finally, as we look at these miracles, we need to see Mark's artistry. Each miracle is presented differently. He does not simply give a list of miracles all in the same format as a less skilled author might do. The first takes place in the synagogue with a crowd of witnesses and involves a dramatic dialogue with the demon about to be expelled. The second is a quiet, gentle affair, taking place in Peter's house, healing his mother in law. The third account brings great crowds of people to the front door and these people were both sick with various diseases and possessed by demons. Jesus heals them all. The final miracle of this chapter is a deeply loving account of a single leper desperate to be cleansed. This man doesn't actually demand healing. He is humble and undemanding but appeals to Jesus' heart: "If you will, you can make me clean." There is no question about Jesus power to heal; the question for the leper is whether he wants to do it. Behind that is probably the leper's experience as a leper: shunned, expelled from society, blamed for his leprosy and treated almost as a non person, one of the living dead. Will Jesus bother with a person like this? Jesus does!

Moving away, then, from the miracles we need to look at the other sections in this chapter. In vv. 16-20 Jesus calls Peter, Andrew, James and John from their fishing boats to come, follow him, and they do so at once. This raises, for us, a host of questions we would like to see answered: did they already know Jesus? Had they heard his teaching before? What happened to their boats and their families? Did they ever go back to fishing? Mark ignores these questions. They are not relevant. Only one thing matters: Jesus calls and they respond at once by following him. That is the message of the whole Gospel. Mark does not give much of the teaching of Jesus. He doesn't go into long biographical accounts of his life. He does not think the hearers of Jesus should sit around having long discussions about the nature of the teaching, or check out the authenticity of the miracles. His one message is, Here is Jesus. Get up and follow him. Disciples of Jesus in the first century when Mark was writing did not have the luxury of time for thought, argument, discussion and uncertainty. The world was coming to an end. The call of Jesus was imperative. Persecution could break out at any time. Get up and go!

In a second interlude between the miracles, in vv. 35-39, we have a very touching scene where Jesus goes out 'a great while before day' and prays. Jesus was a man of prayer or he could not have done the miracles. Behind everything in this Gospel is the long period (about thirty years) when Jesus lived quietly at home and got to know God. We know practically nothing about these hidden years. Later in the Gospel we get brief glimpses of this other side of his life – Mary and his brothers and sisters appearing in Chapter 6; Jesus himself praying in desperation to His Father in the Garden of Gethsemane. Prayer is obviously a central part of Jesus' life, but when the disciples find Jesus praying here, he does not immediately urge them to pray with him. He does the opposite; "Let us go..."

and sets off preaching throughout all Galilee. Jesus is a man driven by an overwhelming sense of mission and by haste to get it done before it is too late.

The final verses of this chapter show us the result of all this preaching and healing: so many people now know about Jesus and want to get near him that he can no longer go openly into a town, but must preach in the country; 'and people came to him from every quarter.' This leaves us with a question that will recur to us throughout the Gospel: Jesus seems to be a brilliant success. He performs miracles; he teaches with authority; people are amazed and astonished by him; they flock to him in such numbers that he gets overwhelmed by them. Why then did he die on a Cross? Why did he end with his mission an apparent failure? Why did all the adoring crowds suddenly abandon him. Was it simply that they never understood?

This makes us wonder whether this was Mark's own experience of preaching the Gospel in the fifties and sixties, twenty years after the death of Jesus. It is such a wonderful Gospel, such amazing news; Jesus was an extraordinary person; in the end he even rose from the dead, and yet the Jewish world he lived in largely ignored him. How can this be? Mark hints at possible answers to these questions but we cannot deal with them here. We are left with a sense of excitement and power driving us on to discover the rest of the story. There is no hint yet that it will end in the disaster, the apparent failure of death on a Cross.

REVOLUTIONARY LUKE

If we were to conduct a poll amongst Christian people as to which was their favourite Gospel the result would probably be a tussle between Luke and John with Luke, perhaps winning. It is easy to see why Luke's Gospel is popular: it includes some of our favourite parables: the Good Samaritan and the Prodigal Son; it tells some of the best stories of the birth and childhood of Jesus; it contains the canticles, Benedictus, Magnificat and Nunc Dimittis; and even the passion story is softened by Jesus' gentle forgiving nature – he says "Father forgive them..." of those who crucified him, and only in this Gospel story do we hear that he forgave one of the thieves on the cross. At the same time Luke's Gospel reads more smoothly than the others. He is well educated (perhaps he really was a doctor and really did accompany the cosmopolitan Paul around the Mediterranean). He writes better quality Greek than the other evangelists and even in English his Gospel reads more smoothly than the carefully constructed John or the tightly written Matthew. It comes as rather a shock to discover that Luke is actually quite a social revolutionary, perhaps the most revolutionary of all the Gospel writers, and that is saying a lot. Mark makes it clear that the coming of Jesus has thrown everything into a confusion which probably presages the end of all things; Matthew takes that further by showing us how the Jews have been superseded by the gentiles ('the last shall be first and the first last' (Matt.20:16)) and his version of the teaching of Jesus in the Sermon on the Mount suggests very different ways of relating to each other than those we know at present. Yet Luke surpasses them all.

More than any other he highlights the role of Mary in bringing the Christ child into the world. Mary wasn't just made pregnant by the Spirit; she had to agree to it. She is absolutely crucial to the salvation story. In a sense most of the great Marian doctrines, and the devotion that has grown up around Mary, find their source in the Annunciation (Luke 1: 26-38). And for Mary read 'women'. In almost every part of Luke's Gospel a story about a man is followed by a story about a woman. It was revolutionary in Luke's time to present women as equal to men. Yet, he goes further in his revolutionary Gospel: it is not just women who are raised up to an unaccustomed height; the first of his canticles contains the verses:

'He has brought down the powerful from their thrones and lifted up the lowly; he has filled the hungry with good things and sent the rich away empty.' (Luke 1:32,33) That verse would please even the most radical Marxist! Luke makes it clear from the start of his Gospel that the new Kingdom's prime concern will be the poor, the weak, the sick: when Jesus emerges from his desert retreat he begins his preaching in Nazareth and reads from Isaiah as a kind of manifesto: "The spirit of the Lord ... has anointed me to bring good news to the poor, to proclaim release to the captives ... to let the oppressed go free." (Luke 4:18,19) Poor people were oppressed both by rich Jews and by the Romans. These were the people who first joined the new Christian Church in significant numbers. Luke has Jesus promising that they will be the ones to inherit the kingdom of God.

Most of us are quite happy with that sort of social radicalism. In the past century particularly we have become used to the idea that the Gospel speaks to the poor and that social inequality is abhorrent to God. We are far from creating a society that reflects this but we do know we should try. Jesus goes further, however, in Luke's Gospel. He challenges the Jewish racism which set the Samaritans apart. A pious Jew would not speak to a Samaritan or let himself be touched by one. Yet this is what the Good Samaritan does. Can we imagine how a committed racist would feel if he were the traveller on the road to Jericho who was attacked by thieves, and a Pakistani, or a black person picked him up and cared for him? Racism has no place in the Kingdom of God, nor does contempt for any of God's people. Tax collectors (publicans) were hated, despised and feared in Palestine for the way they robbed the people. A modern equivalent would be the loan shark. Imagine the story of Zacchaeus with Zacchaeus as a notoriously harsh loan shark, and Jesus goes and eats with him; or Matthew the tax collector actually welcomed into the company of disciples. What if he were a loan shark? Would Jesus not have called him? Or think of tax collector as a Nazi collaborator or a communist informer. It seems Jesus would have brought even one of those into his very mixed company of disciples.

Those are the obviously shocking stories. But others also shock when you think of it. Take the great favourite – the Prodigal Son.

(Luke 15:11-32) We all love the image of the generous Father forgiving the penitent son. Actually the son is not that penitent. There is no sign he regrets the pain he has caused. He has come home to get food and shelter, that's all. Would it not be sensible to keep him waiting till he shows sorrow and understands the nature of his sin? Is he not a challenge to us? When people like him turn up, dirty and smelly at our churches, sometimes during services, do we welcome them as the Father would, or do we ignore them hoping they'll go away? We do want sinners to repent but they need a long period of rehabilitation, socialisation and education before they can really count. I think most of us would be like the older brother, resenting this wasteful young man who is getting all the attention. Yet even to us the Father says 'you are ever with me, and all that I have is yours.'

Or to return to the Passion story, can we be like Jesus and genuinely forgive people even when they hurt us? Society does not do this. Society and the press relentlessly pursue people they think have done wrong. They encourage us to seek justice, by which they mean vengeance and full payout for wrongs received. To stand against that and say we must simply forgive those who wrong us is a very unpopular thing to do. Yet that is what Jesus says, and Luke keeps reminding us of that. It is not easy to forgive when we have been really hurt. I may wish I could do so, but honesty compels me to say I can't. How far I am from being the kind of Christian Luke, or Christ expects me to be!

And then there is the model of the early Christian Church which Luke presents to us in Acts 2:44 where 'all who believed were together and had all things in common; and they sold their possessions and goods and distributed them to all as any had need.' Since Luke wrote long after this time we doubt how far this actually happened. It is clear that Luke thought it ought to happen and his detailed story of Ananias and Sapphira who tried to cheat the Christian community and died as a result shows how important he thought this was. It was, of course, a model for monastic life. It has been the model of Jewish kibbutzim and was tried in small and big ways by various communist societies. It has never been a model for the whole Christian Church, or even single parish churches. One can imagine the opposition there would be to any move to make it so.

We can imagine that Luke, with his concern for the poor and the powerless and his vision of a life of real equality and forgiveness would be a difficult person to live with in today's Christian Church. In fairness to him we should recognise that his Gospel is a really shocking Gospel. If we are not shocked, disturbed, made uncomfortable by our Gospel readings we have probably missed the point of the stories we so love.

FORGIVENESS IN LUKE

"Father, forgive them, for they do not know what they are doing." (Lk 23:34) Those words, spoken by Jesus as the soldiers nailed him to the cross, touch our hearts as they show us a whole new way of encountering the wickedness of other men and women; not anger, not revenge, not threats of divine punishment, not even stoical courage, but compassion. Jesus understands these soldiers, understands their brutality, or their obedience to orders. He sees them as beloved children of God and longs for them to know his Father. Luke puts very similar words on the lips of Stephen when he is stoned to death: "Lord, lay not this sin to their charge." (Acts 7:60) and it becomes almost common in the future for Christian martyrs to forgive their tormentors. In this they only imitate their master. That same master on the cross heard the thief next to him say "We indeed have been condemned justly ... but this man has done nothing wrong ... Jesus, remember me when you come into your Kingdom." and Jesus does not just promise to remember him; he tells him, "Today you will be with me in Paradise." (Lk 23:41ff) He gives him more than he asked for: not just remembrance, not just forgiveness, but eternal life with him, on the basis of a simple confession of sin.

Luke is not the only Gospel writer to make forgiveness a part of the message of Jesus – a glance at the Sermon on the Mount is enough to show that. Yet he gives it a priority that makes his Gospel a message of God's forgiveness. To see how he does this we need to look at three of his best known parables, and one story.

The most famous parable of forgiveness is, of course, the Prodigal Son. It has often been called also the Prodigal Father, because the father is prodigal with his forgiveness. The father doesn't wait for the son to speak his repentance, or show he is really sorry or make promises to behave. He just flings his arms round his son. The coming home was enough. That earned the boy full forgiveness. Or to be more accurate, that made it possible for the father to show that his forgiveness had always been there. It didn't need to be screwed out of him. There was never a time during the boy's absence that the father didn't forgive him; he just needed the son to come home so he could show it. Then he gives far more than the boy asked. The son only asked for a place to sleep and food, and he would work for it. The father restores him to his full rights as a son, and gives a party as well. Whenever we wonder whether we can get God's forgiveness for something we have done, we need to remember that father. God is just the same. The more difficult part is remembering that God is just as forgiving to his other sons and daughters; so we must be too.

A second, much shorter parable is that of the Publican and the Pharisee. The problem there is that the publican or tax collector is not an attractive character. The prodigal son was. Sure, he has behaved badly to his family, wasted a lot of money, committed lots of sins, but in the end we quite like the scamp, especially since he had shown every sign of turning over a new leaf. We can forgive him. The tax collector is different. He is probably a nasty piece of work: he cheats his fellow Jews, acting as an agent for the oppressive Romans. Unlike Matthew or Zacchaeus he hasn't left his tax desk behind him. He hasn't promised to give half his money to the poor. All he has done is admit he is in the wrong. He doesn't even say he is sorry. All he asks for is mercy. You would think God would want some proof of contrition, some promise of amendment, even some sign that he is sorry. But the man only asks for mercy, and he gets it. In the end that is where we are too. No matter how good we have been, how much we have achieved for God, how much we have given away or worked for God, in the end we too will have to stand before the judgement seat and admit that what Christ said would be true, is true; we are unprofitable servants (Lk 17:10). We can't bargain, we can't point out our virtues; we can just ask for mercy, and we will get it. At first sight that may seem rather miserable, that we must just stand there beating our breasts, saying we are miserable sinners. But it isn't like that. God forgives us because he loves us. He forgives us completely because his love for us is complete. And the news that God loves us like that is the most joyful news we can have. That joy will break our hearts.

The third parable is not usually seen as one of forgiveness. It is the Good Samaritan. It seems to be about compassion – a Samaritan showing compassion to a wounded Jew even though they were enemies. That is true. But think what must have gone through the Samaritan's mind. He would often have been insulted by Jews, discriminated against by Jews. We don't know if he knew this Jew to be different. Probably he wasn't. Before he showed compassion he had to forgive the Jew for the wrong done to him so often by other Jews. Compassion makes him do so, and it is one of the factors working in God that makes him forgive. He doesn't see us just as horrible, wicked men and women nor even as miserable, grubby sinners. He sees us as sick children, victims of our condition, victims of other people's example. He understands far better than we do why we sin. He longs to heal us of this horrible disease, and the only way he can do that is by forgiving. Can we receive it?

The next story appears in Luke 7:36-50. It is the wonderful story of a woman, probably a prostitute who gate crashes a dinner party to wash the feet of Jesus. And it ends with Jesus saying "her sins, which are many, are forgiven, for she loved much; but he who is forgiven little, loves little." That is frightening for those of us who feel we don't really commit many sins. It is encouraging for those of us who find as we prepare for confession that the list grows longer and longer. After all the years of Christian life, of prayer and sacraments, still we are full of sin. That is depressing. And yet if we weren't perhaps we wouldn't have the chance to find how much God loves us; we wouldn't realise how much cause we have to love God. In the end we feel sorry for the person who does not think he needs to make his confession. Such a person may never discover just how much God loves.

At the end of Luke's Gospel, just before he leaves his disciples for the last time he tells them that 'the Christ should suffer and on the third day rise from the dead, … repentance and forgiveness of sins should be preached in his name to all nations.' (Lk 24:46) That is the essence of the Gospel as he sees it. If we want to know the real joy of the resurrection of Christ from the dead, we need to repent of our sins; not just in a general kind of way; not even in the long confessions that Cranmer wrote for us and which our modern liturgies have so much watered down. We need to find all those sins lurking in secret corners of our lives and root them out; the more we find, the more appalled we are at just how much is hidden away, the more we shall be amazed at the kindness of God who forgives even these. And the more we shall love him.

LUKE : THE MISSIONARY THEOLOGIAN

When we seek to understand the Gospel of Luke one of the key points we must not forget is that Luke also wrote Acts. Indeed those two books, separated in our Bibles by John are in fact held together in one structure. The story of Jesus begins in Nazareth (Lk 1:26); Jesus begins his ministry in Galilee (4:14) and much of his teaching takes place there. Only in 18:31 does he tell his disciples "see, we are going to Jerusalem..." Jerusalem is where he meets his death, and where he rises from the dead. Unlike the other evangelists Luke has all the resurrection appearances take place in and around Jerusalem. The disciples are specifically told to "stay in the city until you have been clothed with power from on high." (24:49) Acts then takes up the story of how the disciples, now called apostles (1:2 meaning 'those who are sent') receive the Holy Spirit and then immediately start preaching, first in Jerusalem, then led out beyond Judea into Samaria, Antioch in Syria and then on into the Greek world with the Apostle Paul and his companions. Acts ends with Paul in Rome, the centre of the known world. Thus Luke maps out a missionary movement which starts in the rural Jewish area of Galilee, moves to its centre in Jerusalem (where right at the beginning in Chapter One the priest Zechariah learns he will be father of the forerunner John), and then spreads rapidly out of Palestine, through the Greek cities and to Rome, the mistress of the world.

This is no surprise for anyone who has been alert to the priorities Luke gives to the coming of Jesus: in Luke 2:32 the prophet

Simeon describes the child Jesus as "a light to enlighten the Gentiles." As early as Luke 7 a Roman centurion comes to ask Jesus to heal his servant and tells Jesus he does not need to come physically; he can do it from afar. Jesus says, "Not even in Israel have I found such faith." Luke is warning us that the faith of the Gentiles, Greek and Roman, will turn out to be far greater than that of the Jewish people who should have recognised the Messiah. And at the end of the Passion in 23:47 it is the Roman centurion himself who proclaims Jesus' innocence, "Certainly, this man was innocent."

Most of the Gospel story is focused on Jesus and his work of preaching the coming Kingdom; yet in Chapter 10 there is a sudden development. 'Jesus appointed seventy others and sent them on ahead of him to every town …' Whether anything like this really happened in the life time of Jesus is at least doubtful. What is clear is that Luke has turned this story into an idealisation of the mission to the Gentiles. It was brilliantly successful (which Jesus' own mission was not). Jesus says, "I watched Satan fall from heaven like a flash of lightning." That is a triumph over Satan which must surely wait until after the crucifixion. Luke is anticipating the history of Jesus mission: it may seem to have failed as it comes up to the crucifixion, but in fact it succeeded brilliantly after that, as we (and he) know well. Within that same story he hints at what will happen: "Woe to you Chorazin, Woe to you Bethsaida … At the judgement it will be more tolerable for Tyre and Sidon than for you." Gentiles will be saved while Israel is destroyed.

This story of the sending of seventy missionaries provides us with what we might call Luke's own missionary plan.

i. The disciples did not decide on their own to go out and preach the Gospel. They were sent by Jesus. All true mission is inspired by Jesus or by God. Anyone who tries to do mission without keeping that in mind is likely to fail because it will become his or her own project, wrapped up with a personal agenda. Some very talented people have been disastrous Christian missionaries because of their failure to separate their will from God's. Here the emphasis on being sent is crucial.

ii. The disciples do not go out individually but two by two. There are a lot of reasons why this could be so. Clearly it is helpful to support each other and be ready to help each other in times of difficulty or depression. Two people also check on each other to ensure that the Gospel being preached is the authentic one, not a private made up version. And though Luke doesn't quote Jesus, Matthew passes on the saying of Jesus that "where two or three are gathered in my name, there am I in the midst of them." Matt. 18:20. Two people are a witness to the ideal of Christian community.

iii. Jesus does not put much emphasis on their need to preach in words, except that they must announce that the Kingdom of God is coming in the form of Jesus himself. What they must do is "carry no purse, no bag, no sandals" and rely on the people they meet to look after them. And they must heal the sick. That gives us a model for our own attempts at Christian mission. Words do not appear to matter so much, certainly not long sermons. What matters is that we must go as weak, poor representatives of a weak and poor Christ. That in itself is a counter cultural thing to do. And we must care for those we meet, healing (through modern medicine no doubt), giving advice and practical help. We preach the Gospel better by what we do and who we are, than by what we say.

Luke is writing about 60 years after the death of Jesus. Jerusalem has fallen and has been destroyed so that 'not one stone is left upon another.' The temple is gone; the Jewish people have scattered. Luke does not gloat over this destruction of the people of God. But he makes it clear that the followers of Christ are the new Israel. Paul begins his preaching in Jewish synagogues. If they accept him they become the new Christian Church. If they reject him he goes to the Gentiles and they become the new Israel. Increasingly, this becomes the case. Judaism and Christianity go their separate ways, tragically divided worshippers of the same God.

It does seem that the methods set out in Luke 10 are the ones the majority of Christian missionaries actually used in the first century AD. That is a call to us in this century in our concern for mission. And the Gospel preached is the one we have seen: it is centred naturally on the Resurrection of Christ, who is not simply risen from the dead but continually present to people through the Holy

Spirit. Luke does not simply tell a story that happened in the past. It is a story which goes on in the present and is driving men and women into the future. The marks of this new Gospel include the forgiveness of sinners, their restoration to society; it makes a new place for the poor and the weak (the majority of the new converts in the First Century world were indeed poor and weak); and it turns the world upside down.

CHARACTERISTICS OF JOHN

John's Gospel stands out from the Synoptic gospels for its very different style and content. There has been much argument over the centuries whether it is more historical or less, more theological or less, than the other three Gospels. That discussion is one we cannot take up here. What we are concerned with in this chapter is to describe some of the characteristics of John's writing which make his Gospel so fascinating to read.

1. The Signs

Unlike the first three gospels John does not tell of Jesus performing vast numbers of miracles. On the contrary he describes only seven. The fact that there are seven is itself significant as seven is a holy, or complete number. The world was created in seven days. The seven miracles given are:

i.   Turning water into wine at Cana (2:1-11).

ii. Healing the gentile boy (4:46-54).

iii. The healing of the man at the Pool of Bethesda (5:1-9).

iv. Feeding the 5,000 (6:5-14).

v.   Walking on the water (6:16-21).

vi. Healing the blind man (9:1-38).

vii. Raising of Lazarus (11:1-44).

John himself calls these miracles 'signs'; each of them is a sign of who Jesus is, that is, the Son of God. Each miracle develops this theme in a different way. Writers in the time of John loved to structure their work in ways that revealed patterns of significance. So here we have a sign first of Christ's likeness to the creator God, followed by two miracles of healing, followed by two natural miracles demonstrating his authority over material matter and completed with two more miracles of healing, the second of which shows his divine power in having authority over death itself.

Another possible pattern may be discerned linking these signs with the Hebrew Scriptures: The first is a story of creation in parallel with Genesis 1. The second, surprisingly is the healing of a gentile, paralleling Genesis 4-11, which is concerned with the whole world rather than the Jews. Only then does Jesus become concerned with healing and feeding the people of God.

Each of these stories is beautifully crafted, wasting no words, but catching our imagination. Yet at the same time several of them are used as occasions for dialogue, giving the evangelist the opportunity to tell us what Jesus is really doing, and who he is.

2. Characters

Who could forget Nicodemus, or the Samaritan woman at the well, or Mary and Martha? One aspect of John's writing that has always made him attractive to his readers, and hearers, is his description of his characters. Some stories are given at considerable length, allowing the person to be revealed in increasing depth. That is true of the Samaritan woman or the man born blind. Other characters only get a few sentences, perhaps even a few words, yet they are described in clear, deft brush strokes so that they stand out as individuals. So we have the disciples, Peter, Andrew, Philip, Nathanael, the unnamed 'disciple whom Jesus loved'; the friends, Mary, Martha, Lazarus; and the recipients of his grace: the Samaritan woman, the man born blind, the Roman official whose son was healed. Strong as these descriptions are, they never edge Jesus off the canvas. They play a supportive role in the revelation of his divine nature, yet at the same time they are not just cardboard cut-outs. They are real people who must have had well remembered lives in the Christian community. They are, it would seem, ordinary people whose lives were completely transformed by their encounter with Jesus.

3. Literary devices

John did not just write the story of the life of Jesus. He constructed it carefully, rather as a poet may construct a poem. It is designed to be read at different levels. At one level they are simply stories to be told and enjoyed. Like the stories in the other Gospels they show signs of having been told often, and told in a way that made them easy to remember. At the same time John wants to engage his readers in thinking about what these stories really mean, and how they reveal the nature of Jesus as the Son of God.

i.   Step parallelism. When John tells a story it often only gradually reveals the truth he wants to convey. In this it is rather like a person ascending a number of steps until he reaches the top point of his understanding. One of the best examples of this in the story of the man born blind (see below).

ii. Irony. John uses irony in the form that a person says what is actually true about Jesus, but doesn't recognise the truth, and often thinks he is saying the opposite. One excellent example of this is Caiaphas the High Priest who predicts that Jesus will die for the people (11:50). Caiaphas means that Jesus must be got rid of so that the people do not suffer at the hands of the Romans who see Jesus as a potential rebel leader. But precisely because Caiaphas is High Priest he speaks the truth from God, that Jesus will die for the people, to save them and the whole world from sin.

4. 'My father and your Father...'

If there is a single verse that sums up so complex a book as John's Gospel it might be the words Jesus spoke to Mary Magdalene: "I am going to my father and your father, to my God and your God." (20:17) Throughout the Gospel Jesus is presented as the Son of God, and he himself claims that filial relationship along with the special knowledge and special authority that goes with it. Jesus offers this relationship to each of the people he meets in his ministry. Some accept it; others reject it and are judged accordingly. In the final discourses Jesus brings his disciples into his own filial relationship with God.

One result of this which makes John different from the other Gospel writers is his idea of eternal life: for John eternal life starts now. Anyone who has believed in Jesus is already a child of his Father in Heaven.

5. 'The light shone in the darkness…'

John sees many of the critical aspects of life in pairs of opposites; light and darkness (1:5), life and death, truth and falsehood. This does suggest he has a rather gloomy view of life. He speaks often of the world, but usually the world is in opposition to God. Sometimes the world is neutral. Very occasionally it is a place to be saved and brought back into God's care (3:16). Reading John's Gospel can give the impression that he sees the world as a very dark place. He and his Christian community are surrounded by the darkness of persecution, of rejection, of misunderstanding and of heresy. The light comes into the darkness in the form of Jesus Christ, and that light cannot be overcome by the dark but neither can the light finally overcome the dark. The light keeps the followers of Jesus safe until the end comes, and that will be soon.

A feature of John's Gospel is that Jesus makes a number of sayings beginning. 'I am.' These are of great importance as they sketch out both his divine characteristics – "I am the light of the world (8:12), I am the way the truth and the life (14:6), I am the true vine (15:1)," but also his human qualities: "I am the good shepherd (10:11)." Of course, John does not separate his divine from his human characteristics. As God he is perfectly united. John makes clear that all these qualities are already present in Jesus. Anyone who believes in him will find the nourishment, guidance, new life and truth which he or she needs.

6. The sacrifice of the Cross

When Jesus first appears in the Gospel John the Baptist immediately describes him as "the lamb of God, who takes away the sin of the world."(1:29) At the end of the story John underlines this point by using a different chronology from that of the Synoptics. For them the Last Supper is a Passover meal; the lamb has already been slain. John makes it clear the meal is not a Passover meal (13:1 'Before the Passover meal....'). This means that Jesus himself is slain on the Cross about the same time that the Passover lambs were slain. So Jesus himself is the true Passover lamb slain to deliver the people from captivity and to bring them into a reconciled relationship with God.

So when we come to read the Passion story in John's Gospel we find a rather different tone from the others. Jesus is in control. Jesus is offering himself as a sacrificial lamb to take away the world's sin. Caiaphas, the priests, Pilate and the soldiers are all his servants doing his will (though guilty also because they have chosen to do evil). Jesus walks the way of the Cross as one who is ascending his throne. John describes his crucifixion as 'glory'. "The hour has come for the Son of Man to be glorified." (12:23) Jesus' final words on the Cross "It is finished" (19:30) can also be translated "It is accomplished!" It is a cry of triumph: the great work he began by coming into the world has now been completed.

7. The Resurrection

We cannot leave John's Gospel without a look at the way he handles the Resurrection and there are really three stories, each based on a place where the disciples meet Jesus. The first is in the garden by the tomb where Jesus meets Mary Magdalene; the second is the Upper Room where Jesus comes twice to meet his disciples; and the third is by the lakeshore, the main focus of which is Peter who needs to be restored through forgiveness to his position of leadership in the Church.

To understand John's view of the Resurrection we need to go back to Jesus telling them at the Last Supper "I am the true vine..." where it becomes clear that his disciples, all of them, even us, are the branches. We have become part of Christ. We are in him; he is in us. We share in his eternal life already; for us, the Resurrection is already here, even if it is not yet fully present. We live in two worlds. Although John does not use the word 'church' it is the Church as the body of Christ that he is describing. St Paul tells us 'you are the body of Christ and individually members of it.' (1Cor. 12:27) John's imagery of the vine says the same thing.

That is why he can tell Mary Magdalene that his father is now her father; his God is her God. That is why he can give His Spirit to the disciples in the Upper Room so that they can be sent as he was, to spread peace, as he was, and to forgive sins as he did. And finally, in the beautiful tale of Peter's restoration, it is through his love for Jesus that he is given the flock of Jesus, to care for, to feed and in the end to die for.

JOHN 9 – A MAN BORN BLIND

John chapter 9 tells a simple story. A man who is born blind meets Jesus. He doesn't ask for anything but Jesus heals him. As a result of this, much controversy is created among the leaders of the Jews, first as to whether this is a real miracle; second, about the person, Jesus, who did the healing. As a result the man is expelled from the Jewish community and finds his place with Jesus.

John, the writer of the Gospel, has taken this simple story and turned it into a magnificent drama; a drama perhaps, but also a kind of musical symphony. In this one chapter we see most of John's evangelistic concerns appear. His whole Gospel indeed is like a symphony; themes which are raised at the beginning keep appearing, woven and re-woven into different patterns, building up a complex and subtle presentation of teaching and belief. Examining this story in detail will alert us to the themes and concerns of the rest of the Gospel.

Let us start at the beginning:

The disciples ask Jesus, "Who sinned, this man or his parents, that he should be born blind?" This was a question which has troubled the Jewish nation for centuries: do people suffer because they have sinned? Even the great book of Job had not resolved it. Jesus replies, "Neither this man nor his parents sinned, but it was in order that the works of God might be revealed." We would probably agree with the first part of this sentence but find the second part distinctly disconcerting: would God subject a man to decades of blindness just so that his work might be revealed? Yet answering this question is probably not the first thing in John's mind. His whole Gospel is designed to show how the ministry of Jesus reveals the works of God. The entire Gospel only contains seven miracles, but each one reveals an aspect of God's glory, the glory which is shown in Jesus proving him to be God's Son. The question which will be raised in this Gospel is, will people see his glory?

This brings us to the second theme of the story, the contrast between the man born blind, and the people who can see. A man born blind barely exists. He has no name, he cannot be properly a part of society, he must beg for a living; he cannot work. A majority assume that he is blind because of sin, either his own or his parents' and that excludes him from the religious world of Judaism; effectively it excludes him from God, from the covenant of Israel, from the life giving Law. That is where he starts. By the end of the story the man has gained his sight, understood truths the Pharisees could not see, and entered into a saving relationship with Jesus. He has in a sense been created, or born properly for the first time. There are obvious overtones of baptism as being born again (3:3). This blind man has received the gift of rebirth that Nicodemus could not understand.

In verse 4 we have a problem. "We must work the works of him who sent me." Why does Jesus use a plural subject when he appears to be talking about himself? At this stage the disciples, who are a somewhat shadowy group in John's Gospel, are simply following Jesus, listening to him. Later they will do Christ's work: in 14:12

("He who believes in me will do the works I do, and will do greater works…"); in 15:12 ("If they persecuted me they will persecute you; if they kept my word they will keep yours also"); and 15:27 ("you are witnesses"). John is probably directing this to his own contemporaries. After the resurrection they share in the work that Jesus was doing. Here the whole imagery of light and darkness becomes crucial. We have already seen how the blind man is in darkness. Now Jesus says they must work "while it is day", in other words while it is light. "Night comes when no one can work." (3:4) The night is the darkness of evil contrasted with the light who is Jesus. It is the darkness in which the Pharisees and all unbelievers are shown to be. It is the darkness that comes at the end of the world, which John and his Christians are expecting to happen soon. It gives urgency to the whole story. Against the darkness is Jesus who now says "I am the light of the world." (9:5).We have heard that already in 1:9,10 and 8:12. It is a favourite Johannine theme. We will hear it much further developed in 12:35,36 when Jesus tells the disciples they themselves have this light and must use it. It reflects also Isaiah 9:2, 'The people who walked in darkness have seen a great light' and Isaiah 49:6, 'I will give you as a light to the nations.' Throughout his Gospel John evokes the themes of the Jewish Scriptures to show that Jesus is their fulfilment.

Having made his claim to be the light of the world Jesus now proves it by spitting on the ground, making mud and anointing the blind man's eyes. The blind man washes and can see. The little action of making mud becomes a cause of controversy. Making mud was one of the things you could not do on the Sabbath. Jesus deliberately breaks the Sabbath not just in healing the blind man, but in the way he did it. Possibly also this action is meant to recall Genesis 2:7 where 'The Lord God formed man from the dust of the ground.' Jesus shares in the creative activity of God, since he is himself God and his creative activity is not just to heal a blind man, but to restore the blind man to the human race, to make a real person of him. And why does Jesus specify the pool Siloam? This is the pool which would have been used for purification during the feast of Tabernacles described in Chapter 7. John uses the pool to knit his story into what has gone before. Light in the darkness was a major strand of the Tabernacles festival and is evoked here.

John is a brilliant story teller and knows how to vary his style. In a few verses he has disposed of the theory that sin causes blindness; he has identified the work of Jesus (and that of the disciples) with the work of God; he has introduced light and darkness, claimed Jesus as the light of the world. Now he carefully describes how Jesus performs this healing. The actual healing comes in just a few words (seven in the Greek), 'Then he went and washed and came, seeing' (9:7) The sheer brevity and simplicity of this account makes it effective as a description of the power of God.

Jesus withdraws from the scene and most of the rest of the chapter describes the Jews questioning the man who was blind in order to find out what has happened. Here John skilfully weaves together two different themes with two contrasting movements. On the one hand we have the Jews, beginning with the bystanders and rapidly moving on to the Pharisees, asking what has happened. The bystanders question whether this really is the beggar, and are divided about it (v.9). They ask how he was healed and the beggar tells them. (v.11) They take him to the Pharisees. The Pharisees ask how he was healed and he repeats the story. The Pharisees say Jesus can't be a good man because he broke the Sabbath. (v.16) Once again there is division amongst them because some think he must be a good man to have healed the blind man. The Pharisees again question whether it is the same man and call in his parents, who confirm this is their son. By now the Pharisees have abandoned reason and simply insist that Jesus is a sinner (v.24) and try and force the beggar to agree. He refuses. For them the story ends at v.40 when they ask, "Surely we are not blind?" In fact they were.

Meanwhile the beggar is moving in the opposite direction. In verse 11 he describes his healer simply as "a man called Jesus." By verse 17 when asked who he thinks Jesus is he says firmly, "He is a prophet." By verse 33 he has gone further and now says "If this man were not from God he could do nothing." From there it is a short step to when he meets Jesus and says "Lord, I believe" and worshipped him. It is part of John's artistry that he brings the man from a simple knowledge of the man Jesus, to the recognition that he is the Son of God without any awkwardness in the telling. And the irony is that it is the sceptical questioning by the Pharisees who are trying to convince him that Jesus is a bad man which brings him to a deeper and deeper knowledge that Jesus really is from God.

John is well known for his irony, and this story is full of it. The fundamental story is ironic, that an ignorant, blind beggar from the very bottom of the social heap should be the one to teach the well educated Pharisees about God. In v.8 those who knew the beggar perfectly well when he was blind can't recognise him now he can see. It seems that they have lost their sight just as he has gained his. There is irony in the remark of v.16 that Jesus could not be from God since he did not keep the Sabbath. In fact Jesus was God, and had made the Sabbath so he was not bound by its laws. In v. 24 the Pharisees tell the blind man "Give glory to God…" This was supposed to be an oath to tell the truth. The irony is that the man does give glory to God through his healing and continues to give glory by testifying who Jesus really is. As the Pharisees go on and on seeking the truth of the story they seem in fact to grow more blind. As it becomes clearer and clearer that this man really is the man born blind, and that he has really been healed, they seem less and less able to accept either truth. The darkness that formerly filled the blind man's life is steadily descending on them. Eventually the blind man himself loses patience and turns irony, or more accurately, sarcasm on them, "Do you also want to become his disciples?" (v.27)

To become a disciple of Jesus was to lose one's place in the Jewish community. The Gospel has warned us of this already in the story of Nicodemus who must come to Jesus by night. In this present story we find the parents of the blind man reluctant to say the obvious thing about Jesus in case they were thrown out of the synagogue. When the beggar persists in his witness to Jesus he is thrown out by the Pharisees. There is in fact no evidence that people were excluded from the synagogue during the time of Jesus. It certainly happened later on when a formal decree of excommunication was made soon after the fall of Jerusalem. It had evidently impinged hard and bitterly on John and his community as it is referred to again in 12:42 and 16:2. Indeed the whole tenor of this Gospel, deeply and increasingly hostile to the Jews, because of their hostility to Jesus, speaks of the bitter experience John has known of being expelled by his own people. It is clearly for this reason that Jesus, who has disappeared from the scene during the blind man's questioning, reappears as soon as he is expelled. Back in 6:37 Jesus has promised "Whoever comes to me I will not cast out." Now he comes and finds the blind man and asks if he believes in the son of man. Son of man in the Gospel can simply mean Jesus himself (rather than an apocalyptic son of man figure). However, in John the main function of the son of man is 'to draw all men to himself.' (12:32) The man once blind comes out of the Jewish community, leaving behind his former friends and even his parents who have chosen (like so many Jews in John's own day) to sit on the fence and not admit to what is obvious about Jesus. He is now welcomed into the new community of faith which is formed around Jesus. Jesus himself then passes judgement on the Jews; not only are they blind, but they who had accused both him and the blind man of being sinners are themselves in sin. (v.41)

There is much else that could be drawn out of this story to show its Johannine characteristics. we will content ourselves with four further points:

In the passage just referred to Jesus says "It is for judgement that I have come into this world." (v.39) This would appear to contradict what he says in 3:17 "God did not send the son into the world to judge the world..." In fact that same passage continues, "He who believes does not come to judgement; he who does not believe is judged already." So clearly in v.39 it is the presence of Jesus that compels people to make a choice that will bring judgement on themselves, or not. That choice is whether or not to believe that he is from God.

This brings us to the second point, the importance of belief. The phrase 'you believe,' either as question or statement, occurs 16 times in John's Gospel. For John this is the crucial test for a Christian; not moral behaviour, not keeping the law, but believing in Jesus. That is what makes a person a part of the community of the saved.

The third point concerns the Jews. Throughout the Gospel they appear in varying degrees of hostility to Jesus and his followers. Yet they are not united. In 9:9 some say the healed man is the blind man; others say he is not. In v.16 some Pharisees say he must be a sinner since he broke the Sabbath; others say he cannot be a sinner if he did such a miracle; 'and there was division among them.' The same has happened in 7:43 when the Jewish people at the Feast of Tabernacles argued whether this really was the Christ. It happens again in 10:19 when they are divided as to whether Jesus is possessed by a demon or not. Jewish communities have always been notoriously argumentative. In John's own time, as in Jesus' time, they may as a whole have rejected Jesus, but there were clearly considerable elements within the community arguing about the significance of Jesus.

And finally one must attend to the brilliance of the structure of John's story. As with all the Gospel writers, John is a consummate story teller and constructs his story so well that the careful structure itself does not stick out. The story begins with seven verses in which Jesus is the lead actor; it ends with seven verses in which again he is the centre. In between he is not physically present though he is constantly talked about. The story itself begins with blindness and ends with blindness. So we find that Jesus and blindness are the two frames of the story. Yet at the beginning it is the beggar who is blind; at the end it is the Pharisees who are blind. The whole story is structured round this contrast between the blind beggar and the Pharisees. So we find that on three occasions the blind man humbly confesses his ignorance (vv.12, 25, 36), yet in the end he is the one who knows. Meanwhile the Pharisees on three occasions state what they know about Jesus (vv. 16, 24, 29): twice that he is a sinner, and once that they don't know where he comes from. They are wrong on the first two and the third is their judgement.

In the end we must see this story as one of darkness and light. The darkness is the story of the Jews, who meet Jesus, see his works, discuss it at great length, but in the end, for the most part, reject him and choose the blindness which is sin, and leads to death. On the other hand are the smaller number of people who begin in darkness but find their way out into the light where they find Jesus and are brought into the community of brothers and sisters around Jesus. That in brief is the whole story of John's Gospel, mapped out in the Prologue (1:1-18), beginning with the preaching of John the Baptist and ending with the disciples having breakfast with Jesus on the seashore.

MARY IN JOHN'S GOSPEL

Mary the Mother of Jesus appears only twice in John's Gospel: once at the beginning of the Gospel – she is indeed the first woman to appear; and once at the Cross which could be taken as the end of the human part of the story of Jesus. In each case her appearance is brief yet full of significance.

Mary at Cana

The story starts as what looks like a perfectly normal human affair. A couple are getting married. Their wedding party, according to local custom would have lasted seven days. Towards the end of the feast they ran out of wine. That would be very embarrassing. We may guess that this family was closely related to Mary and she feels some responsibility to avoid the embarrassment this could cause. So she asks Jesus to do something about it with consequences we know well.

The first surprising thing is that Mary is mentioned first, 'and the mother of Jesus was there.' (v.1) Only afterwards are we told that 'Jesus and his disciples were also invited to the marriage.' Mary is not referred to by name either here or in 19:25, but by the title 'mother of Jesus'. This is, of course, an honourable title for any woman in the Middle East who has had a son, and that is true throughout Africa as well.

The dialogue in this passage is full of ambiguity. Mary makes the first statement, "They have no wine." On the face of it this could be a mere statement with no expectation that Jesus will do anything about it. On the other hand the Synoptic tradition certainly believed that Mary knew from the start that Jesus was from God. Does John think that too? Certainly in this story Jesus himself seems to think Mary is expecting something from him.

Jesus' reply is similarly ambiguous: his address of Mary as 'Woman' is not in the least bit impolite or curt (as English readers often think). It is unusual though for a son to address his mother so. He also appears to refuse the implied request ("My hour is not yet come") although he then goes on to do what he is asked. What is probably at stake here is John's own agenda to make it clear throughout the Gospel that Jesus acts only on his own free choice to do the Father's will. He is not under Mary's control, and his calling her 'woman' rather than 'mother' may have been to distance him from the obligations of family relationship, as happens in a different incident in the Synoptic tradition. (Matt 12:46ff, Mark 3:33ff, Luke 8:19ff) Yet Mary was persistent in the face of an apparent refusal, as was the Roman official later in 4:49, and she tells the servants to do whatever Jesus asks. From then on the focus moves to Jesus and Mary does not reappear until the Cross. It is in the light of that appearance that we need to understand the events at Cana.

John's Gospel is very carefully structured. Each person has an important part to play; each story is placed at a point in the story of Jesus which is theologically important. Mary stands as a pair of brackets, or bookends at the beginning and end of Jesus' ministry. This alone underlines her importance.

Mary at the Cross

The Gospel began with the account of how the Word, who 'was God', became flesh. Now we meet the woman through whom the Word became flesh. Mary is not simply the mother of the earthly Jesus. She is, as the Greeks loved to call her, 'Theotokos', the God-bearer, or the Mother of God.

So as we meet her standing at the foot of the Cross we remember she is not there simply in her tragic role of the mother of this Jesus dying a horrible death. She is there because she was chosen by God to do the most important thing a woman (or, indeed, a man) has been asked to do in the whole history of the world, to give the Son of God flesh and to be his mother.

In this story we start with the obvious point: Mary is Jesus' mother, and it is the role of a son, especially the eldest son, to care for his mother. In the midst of his suffering Jesus thinks of others. In Luke's Gospel he thinks of the soldiers and the penitent thief. In John's Gospel he thinks of his mother. He asks his most loved disciple to care for her after his death.

Yet we are concerned here not just with what actually happened at the foot of the Cross, but how John understood that. John never names the beloved disciple. Does he stand here for all disciples? From its earliest times the Church has understood this story to mean that Mary was given into the care of all the disciples of

Christ, that is the Church itself. She has remained important to the Church because Jesus wanted it so. Her images, statues and stories are cherished in the Church because Jesus wanted us to cherish her. And as the Beloved Disciple became her son, so do we all become her sons and daughters. We are brothers and sisters of Christ. In John 20:17 Jesus tells Mary Magdalene: "I am ascending to my father and your father; to my God and your God." He is sharing his father and God with all of us, but he has already shared his mother.

The significance of Mary in this Gospel gains further layers of meaning from the account in Revelation 12. Here a woman 'clothed with the sun' brings forth a child who is swept up into heaven while the woman flees into the desert to escape the wrath of the great dragon which is eventually thrown down by Michael. Although Revelation was not written by the same person as the Gospel, it probably came from the same circle of disciples. This woman, like Mary was a key figure in the drama of salvation. She is also a counterpart to Eve in Genesis 3, only here she is rescued from the serpent unlike Eve who gives in to him. Generally this woman is taken to represent the people of God who are being protected in the midst of persecution. Yet John's writings are full of multiple significances, and the fact that this woman is simply called 'woman,' as in John 2 and John 19 makes an obvious link. Just as Jesus was for Paul and the early Church the second Adam (Romans 5:14, 1 Cor. 15:22) so Mary was quickly seen to be the second Eve. At Cana though, instead of tempting the Second Adam away from the father's will, she seems to indicate where he is to begin. At the Cross, instead of being banished from the garden to labour with

Adam at the hard task of bringing up a family, she is given a vast human family and honoured as the mother of them all.

This is not a fanciful understanding of the story since on both occasions when the Mother of Jesus appears in John's Gospel, she is closely associated with the disciples, and given a mother's role with the apostle John. In Revelation she is shown to have 'other children' whom the devil now persecutes. So later interpreters have taken her here and in John 19 as a symbol of the Church that protects its own in this 'last time' of persecution.

What we see actually in this sorrowful scene of Mary at the foot of the Cross are the birth pangs of the new people of God of whom Mary is the Mother.

AND FINALLY … JESUS!

Jesus said, "I am the way, the truth and the life." (Jn.14:6.) That means that Jesus is at the heart of Christian religion. That is a very obvious thing to say, but it does often get forgotten. People talk about Christianity as if it is all about the Church, or moral behaviour, or doctrines or even the Bible. Christianity is about all these things and they are all important but they derive their importance from Jesus and are meant to get us in touch with Jesus and the amazing things he did for us.

St Mark begins his Gospel, 'The beginning of the Gospel of Jesus Christ, the Son of God.' As we read his Gospel it becomes clear that Mark does not regard the Gospel as being the teachings of Jesus, or even the acts of Jesus. The Gospel *is* Jesus. What matters is how we respond to him. Do we accept him or do we reject him? Above all, do we answer his call to "Come, follow me"?

Actually, Jesus himself would probably say the Gospel is not primarily about him, but about his Father, God. He tells us in John 14 that "I and the Father are one… He who has seen me has seen the Father." That was his task on earth, to show people the Father. And showing them the Father's love led him to be crucified.

So when we come to read Scripture our first task is to discover Jesus, or to find God. This we can do in a host of different ways. It may be through the monastic process of 'Lectio Divina' – a quiet meditative reading of Scripture, chewing over the phrases and verses rather like a cow chewing the cud until the deepest meanings come to us. It may be through imaginative contemplation: building up a picture, or a story of what we read so that its real significance can come home to us. Sometimes we will relate to Christ through our feelings. Sometimes it will be through the intellect. We mustn't forget the intellect. As Anglicans we are committed to a Christianity that embraces faith and reason. Time spent studying Scripture with a commentary will deepen our faith and enrich our commitment to Christ.

Jesus also said, "Where two or three are gathered in my name, there am I among them." (Matt.18:20). Most often it is right to study, meditate or pray through Scripture on our own. It is also good to do it with others. Jesus never intended Christian life to be a solitary experience. "I am in my Father, and you in me and I in you." (Jn. 14: 20) That means we will meet all the other Christians who are in Jesus. They are part of our story and we are part of theirs. Reading Scripture together is an adventure, a journey, a pilgrimage. It should always be exciting!